A Boy in The City

A Boy In
The City

Poems

S. Yarberry

DEEP
VELLUM

Dallas, Texas

Deep Vellum Publishing
3000 Commerce St., Dallas, Texas 75226
deepvellum.org · @deepvellum

Deep Vellum is a 501c3 nonprofit literary arts organization
founded in 2013 with the mission to bring
the world into conversation through literature.

ISBN: 978-1646051786

Library Of Congress Control Number: 2022932157

Cover design by Kayla E. | designaltar.org
Typesetting by www.ineedabookinterior.com

Printed in the United States of America

TABLE OF
CONTENTS

CHAPTER

CHAPTER

But of course, there is a movement—

       cum and fog—

              revolution without beginning. How does one
              achieve eternal bliss? By saying: Mr. Mr. in the plainest
              of language. I occur. A cat meows. I want the heart of
              a tree when it has been raining. I want a stupendous
              smugness, and the self— as gentle as concern—
              to dispense its terrible truth.

I have sought for a joy without pain,

For a solid without fluctuation.

Why will you die, O Eternals?

Why live in unquenchable burnings?

—from *The Book of Urizen* by William Blake

THE
HISTORY

In the midst of the night—
you put your lips to the bare
of my back.
When your mouth is agape
it's the start to a cave,
the shape of an opal—
Inside your mouth
lives something to say, though
you don't say it. We live this way.
Your hand grabs
at my thigh, my hip. You sleep
and I wake—
I think in the night, before
the blankness takes back over:

> *Lover this, lover that.* Opulent
> gossip, circulates, through
> the institutional hallway.
> I see a crow: *crow!* I say.
> Nobody cares. Which is more
> than fine— there's a note
> on my desk, reads: *I'd steal a horse*
> *for this*. For this? I think.
> Good God! Hazard Adams is
> droning on about Blake's
> "thoughtless hand" being somehow
> mechanic— like the seasons,

the planets. Can the universe

be mechanic? It bothers me.

Anyways, your

thoughtless hand— brushes

across my breast, the breast

I hate. Except you don't

kill me in this poem— If I am

the fly, then I survive. Survive?

There's something about me

that is falling fast asleep.

If the universe decides to take me—

I hope it swallows me whole.

LIPS CRASH
WITH LIPS,
INEVITABLE

A modern catastrophe, we are, you and I. Blowing smoke
into the wind, napping on the couch. Rain hits the windows.
I doze in and out. Wet tires on the wet street. I dream
of peaches that hang like lanterns
in the dark. This is what we want: sex, then rest. Sex,
then rest. Anarchy, then composure.

You have another lover, who lives out of state. When she
texts you— I think: *Oh nuts! my heart is so breakable.* A siren
starts— a fire truck glowing in the storm. Later, we'll drink beers.
Our friends will wage themselves into the air. I have another love too,
u kno— it's hard to be alone. It's hard to be in love two-fold. How bizarre.

Barnacles are dying. How horrible to watch your life
go by and want so much. Those purple mountains, rough—
mouths agape. You wake me up— we kiss.
Ask: *What're we going to do today? What're we going
to do?* My whole life ignites. *We'll do it all. Everything.*

CITY-BUILDERS

When your body meets my body
the world goes blank, we build
a new landscape— we call each structure
New New New then *Work-In-Progress*.
The pastoral lies somewhere beyond
the skyline. We've broken sweat.
We call each other "yes, yes" then
"don't stop" then "don't leave."
We have new names, or our names
are new to us again. You pick
beetles and I pick rays to inhabit the city,
safe from extinction and then we play
a real game, where we pick
fallen hairs off one another's bodies—
who's who— both dark and in varying
lengths. I don't have the words
for what we are building. Not exactly.
But the buildings have purpose
even if they're not all homes.
I am saying this city is untouched, unseen,
or unforeseen. I am saying you touched
me somewhere I cannot explain or locate.
I call you *you* and you call me *you* and once
we sat on the fire escape sweating
in the early heat of May, we filled
our mouths with beer from gold cans,

smoke thick thick thick, bright tongues,

slick lips, fingers to suck like

hard candies. Anything else than the word,

we know, we should say.

Instead, we sit and listen to the sound

of some structure, a few blocks

down, get its walls busted in. Naming

it in our head *New New New*.

Your hand brushes my knee.

THE
LOVERS

I once knew everything—
fish in clear water, a name
in the back of my throat.

I thought of beauty,
constantly, in those days.
It was tragic and romantic

the way I moved—drinking
warm rum and running
my hand up your thigh.

Close, then closer,
was my motto. Until
a moment did us in.

It's a game, though,
this knowing. You know,
you know, you know—

then that cool rush
of oblivion. *You must
know this:*

what it is to doubt. A sad
sack jacking off

into a winter night.
I consider a word.
Occulatae: L. meaning
"equipped with eyes."

If I could know
what I needed to know—
I wouldn't be here

with the house plant
dying, watching snow
fill the neighbor's yard.

You, this very thing I fear,
are exactly what I want.
The sun goes under water.

Something emerges. What is it?
What is it that I want to know?
It's an idea, I think, a stone.

You, I said, though,
of course. Was I lying?
I know I have lied before.

Days pass like perfume into the air.

Fear eats at you like a dog. There's

a dog in the neighbor's yard. You listen

as the bus comes and goes and comes

and goes. You call this: keeping time.

There was once a harbor, in your childhood,

the harbor kept expensive boats

and strange animals. Occasionally

a big fish, a seal, a dolphin. There was nothing

safe about the harbor, though you were

told it was so. When you entered the

harbor it felt like anything, anything

at all, could hurt you. And then

you felt like that all the time. There's a noise

in the other room. There is always

something that should not be, being,

being and won't be stopped.

STAGE
DIRECTIONS

A world of fragment is my private life.
A world, though, is just the world to the public.
If my life is a field then it's a dirt field.
Regular, and bearing all dragged through it.
Marked, is what I mean. The dirt harrowing.
Now, I'm all about the exterior. Earnestly,
here: the day's great sweat: full throttle
and fragrant—the sky dark like an animal's
eye. Odd fruit at odd angles. A small dog
barking. Rain coming down. Street lights.
A stack of bricks for no good reason.
In another room you read Perec, touching
your own gold sorrow like a pet. *Get used
to using each other*, one guy once said.
The wind rubs through trees. Dumpsters
like bad urns upon the asphalt. I drink
a spritzer. A night time spritzer. This is all
for the public. All of it. Inside, though, think:
course-core-coarse-corps-body-death.
The drink going down cool.
The rain coming down like a violence.

MEDUSA

I flipped. I flipped out. The world wanted something from me,
so I burst through the doors! Here's my naked chest (ooh-la-la).
Here's my anatomical anonymity blushing in a burst of blue light!
Which is all to say, I framed myself in the window, grotesque
and chewy like another damn Picasso painting.

My nipples hardening against

the glass.

I watch myself get fucked hard in the back of a car—fast-forward,
pause, play, play, repeat. I call this: *the momentum of my life*!
As the figure in my mind comes into view now, roadside attraction,
the mind recognizes something simple: *pig   pig*. A circle,
but more fucked up. In the mornings, I get dressed in a festoonery
of manhood. Coat. Buttons on the left. When pig comes into view
she's like a stain of womanhood upon my horizon. Horrendous?
Horrendous. Thick skin. In the mornings the parrots come, chaotic.
A mouthful of curse words, curtains. Oh, I'll tell you about a complicated
man, a man with curves so soft I have wished to bring my lips
to his shoulder and weep. What I have learned from pig:
All possibility is heavy on the ground. We all know the story—where
the pig eats the child. Horrendous? *Horrendous*. Oh animal, animal,
wherefore art thou? I'll admit it: I've wanted to break to pieces in your mouth.

*

Gosh-darn! Lickety-split! There's something pink and hulking outside
my window. I write the figure love songs and try to seduce it. By seduce

I mean bring it inside where no one can see us—my medusa,
my end-of-times. The story goes: there was something sick in my
barnyard. The story goes: there was something so pretty in my
barnyard. The story goes erratic and then off the rails. The story goes:
I wanted to hurt myself in my barnyard. The story goes: there's
something wrong in my barnyard. The story goes and goes . . . what is
for certain is that pig is in the barnyard whether she wants to be
or not. The figure does come inside—pig and I? We have met
many times. When the mood is right, we spill like first light.
Untouchable and everywhere and illuminating.
It's your barnyard, pretty boy, she laughs—
where do you hide your pigs?

SELF-PORTRAIT
(PUNCHING BALL)

I am. I am. I am an invention.
A head stripped to muscle.
When I take apart an image—
a self comes into view. Candle.
Omelet. Pile of hair. There
were times of laughter. I built
a mote of birds around my house
and drooled for protection—safety
behind the uncanny. Ah! a force—
so cruel, it took me. Weeps fell
from my mouth like crumbs. Silence
hit the tin drum of my torso.
Once, I had a paradise. The paradise
crumbled like watching an animal
snap in two. The paradise crumbled
like watching a man become his idea.
If I could be your David, I wouldn't
be able to move. A precious rumor—
that I had a face. I had nothing.
There is nothing you can have from me.

OF FIGURE
AND FIELD

On the phone you say:
I wish I could forgive you,
but I can't. I stare across
my apartment. There's
a bowl a girl had given me—
appalled at my lack
of kitchenware. It's white
and blue and thin.
I shudder at the rotten
emptiness that any bowl,
especially this bowl,
today, prompts.
There is no such thing
as forgiveness—
the shadow of error
is terribly permanent.
How can this be?
That it isn't us
sitting there on the ridiculous
beach— with our naked
thighs pressed together,
tragically in love—
the whole city
some sweeping mess behind us.
Who cares? I keep thinking.
Slur of nights.

A car alarm starts. It's almost funny,
the gravity of loss, in moments like these.
The phone hums against my desk,
it's not you, I tell myself—
bewildered and undone, *not you*.
The air is so crisp,
the radiator so loud,
I cannot even forget that I am alive,
I am here, right now, I am missing you.
Come back.

CORYDON
TO
ALEXIS

I follow you through that friend's awful pause
before telling me how you've been. *Each creature
is led by that which it most longs for*— which is to say

you pull me through these awful days where the only heat
is a lonely one. I imagine you in your coat,
both of us young, excited and stripping

little lambs all abloom and stupid
in the stupid night. Alas alas
what have unhappy I been hoping for?

This is a dead-end trade: my time
for the hopes of yours. It ends *There'll be another.*
But I live in the woods, there are no other songs

here, there are no others. When I belonged to you,
my-Alexis, during that cold-close winter,
we were the moon and the stars
those nights—both foot and shadow.

We were the city booming. The trees? There were none.

Enter the house. The house that's pink.

Place your palm on the wall and cringe

at the texture of paint. A shiver runs

through your body, your back. Turn

your head. She is standing there

in the hallway. She walks closer to you.

You're nervous, but it's what you want.

Her red lips on your neck, mouth. Her

hands unbutton your shirt then unbuckle

the bright silver of your belt. Geckos

are watching your every move from

behind the unblinking gloss of eyes.

It's what you want. She's fucking you

hard. In and out and in and out. It feels

good. It feels like what you want. Late

night traffic. Tides.

SPHINX

I want to pick stoplights like apples,
and call all green bulbs pears.

Okay,

the streetlights are city-tulips, blooming against the coming night.

There is nowhere else to be. Not tonight—

and the sky is what some call violet, but I call it

the blue-lipped death that settles behind the dark cast
of empty trees in this horrific evening hour.

How do you see me anyways? This comes from the gut.

I want to flip
over rocks and cars
and call them doorways.
Somewhere else to slip into.

The sky cannot hold. Not like this. Molded clouds clot
the air— pregnant with water or fire or something mean.

There's a devil on my shoulder
and he is singing a funny song

and it's getting stuck in my head.

Oh Nobodaddy!
Oh Ghostobody!
Oh Good-GoddO!

And you are missing. From all of this:
The streets, and the lights, and the strangers.
There is no you in any of it.

Good-bye sticks to me
like ticks on a deer. And I hate all the words I have— each one
cannot get to you.

Everyone is alone out here, but at least no one seems angry. The strangers
wear running shoes
and other practical garments— walking home or somewhere close. Their
coats shining
when the headlights touch too hard.

How easy to be someone else, I lament to no one in particular. My shoulder-
devil, perhaps,
is eavesdropping ....

Car doors slam like shouts!

good-night, good-good-night

When the street is doused in white, so untouched I find it hard to look at,
how do I see anything else? How do I get back to where I meant to be?

There was a road. I want you to answer me. You were just out of reach.

AUTOMANIA

I walk upon the proscenium— shout:
    I AM UNCOMFORTABLE
    IN THIS CURRENT FORMATION
Or proclaim, I should say. I proclaim it.

The simple things are as follows:
It is October. The sky is grey
and thick like a woolly sheep!
We are shepherds of our own
making. Rain— de minimis.

Abstraction isn't *useful*,
but it is, and we use it.
We are lovers,
and we are.

I sit around, today, thinking to my-self:
    This blushing Ichor
    covets 2 b mine,
    or, my origin.
This is my oneiric-self. Not my generic-self.

This, for instance, is my formal-self:
    Does my body elude you, or, seduce you?

I stand each morning as an unknown entity.

Not formless, but formidable.

Language is a parapet,
just as my body is a parapet.
If a word is a barricade to meaning—
then how do we say?

This is: corporeal,
not corpse, but soft.

What I mean: I stand each morning
on the daily stage. When I say shout— I mean look.
The reflection? Something so fantastical
that I cannot believe I hate it.

DOWN
BELOW

How can I write this
when I'm afraid
to think about it?
            —Leonora Carrington

The world around me
didn't crash—it jammed.
A car broken down. Slow
sputtering, then
that ultimate-fail. Even
in nightmares, I learned
there were lemons,
toilettes, shared cigarettes.
When I asked for help
there was no help.
I wore a blue dress.
Sometimes I did as I was told.
The woman in red stockings—
her hair pulled back
in braided horns—smiled,
through it all. I was transfixed.
The world was ending—
I saw it everywhere—this ending.
I destroyed myself,
running from rain. I couldn't
tell you who was who anymore.
Eitherway, I was erotic.
I was not to be believed.

THE
CAVE

Inside the cave is a cavern and soon
the cavern becomes cavernous, carnivorous. Someone
points. Cranium, says *crane*. A bird unbends its neck
from its white ovaled torso. Squawks. Flies and flies, forever,
off into the pale, pale, pale . . .
Inside the cave, the word of it, we get "turned on,"
we blush, we try to crawl inside each other's bodies.
We sit like this until one of us disappears.

THE
WOLVES

My mind once
opened like a jowl. Jaw hung
      loose from skull.
Today, though,
      my head feels
like a swarm-o-swans. It feels
      imperfect, impertinent.
The curves of birds
      dapple my drainpipe.
Shreds of sentences approach
      a portrait   torn
in the eye   dewlap
      dripping from the blades
of grass   handjobs playing inside . . .
      Filth is nothing new.
I open my head like a variety
      show. Anything goes.
A horror that started off abstract
      becomes utterly real. Thick
the skin of an utter entered my hand.
      Oh pain, Oh death, Oh Oh
          observation.
Everything feels like a rickety homestead.
      The horror being a what?
The moribund experience of knowledge
      entered me. The green hump

of the bridge is forever behind

us. A school of dreams shine

in shallow waters—silver then blue

then back again. The light seems

to come from nowhere. A dream, a dream,

then the perfect morning. *I don't know*

what are a body and hands

a mouth a sex

I don't know where you went. Outside

the window there is a sky.

Outside, of myself, I set down a glass

of water. The day is provoking

comprehension. Two rabbits, I notice,

two squirrels, me doubled,

then doubled again. Where was it

that I was looking? Or, where

was it that I was looking for? There's

no such thing as a gilded memory—

I'm sitting here open minded. Wolves

come into view. What do they want?

They want me, I just know it.

The lamp is a silver teapot

and outside a large white van is parked.

She comes home—she runs

her fingers through your hair

and kisses you. She kisses you

until you fuck her. You're so depressed.

Back then you were so depressed.

You never wanted anyone to touch you,

not even her. How do you tell that to someone?

You don't. It builds like a jetty between you.

REQUIEM
CIRCUIT

I move through this city—
an eternal disruption. The air
shawling and pewter and wet.

The catalyst is always the body
in motion. I move as a tear,
as in terror. Interrupt

into rupture. I I I false pillar
of history. I admit: I'm tumbling.
There was a time this meant
to dance with contortions—
it's fond to think that way—
history, a simple epic memory:
contorted and queer and yours.

Human argument,
human integument

waiting for grass to puncture
a face too soft to bear. Verbal
cues and car windows create
thy form so flaccid and false,
or faulty— I should say.

I was afraid

and I was always that.
Trapped in what could be
and never was.

Cattails frill a childhood.
Seals bark in the nighttime.
The soul— a slippery fish. A thought
so mighty that it surmounts
my wild grasp.

ICARUS

her shape— is buoyant
against:

    * NIGHTTIME CITY-GLITZ *

building-lights bud the ramifying skyline

(her shoulder? pearling
in the half-light)

                        Sure, days pass,
debris falls

we clean / we say: *Good Morning!*

Her eyes collect like stillicide,
perpetual, upon her face.

How do we do this?

(((silence)))

What am I if not a broken boy?

THE
SCHOLAR

The sentence became a medium
for desire to traverse, then a livelihood
began to take place. The difference
was all in the performance. I dress up,
at night, and watch the bugs
fuck beneath the porchlight. I wish to end
it all. It rains. It rains again.
There's an exhaustive sort
of brutality to my life. A mundane existentialism
that leans in close to the death clatter
of that epistemic grid of what it means to be
another undone suicide. I put the television on,
a show—radiant theater of sitcoms
where "suicide" does not exist.
The hard word. The concept. The oblivious object.
An addiction, this idea. *If I enter the myth, what*
desires will I have to fill? I find myself
asking. Asking again. I have often needed to save my life.
A methodology to my existence, is desirable,
something excruciatingly formal. I speak
in polemics eternal and infernal. It's not
really playful—the ending of my life—
though theatrics are certainly involved.
Ah, to cohere to the world we make
ourselves up in. I twirl my arm around
like a windmill, a chainsaw. I pray

to Aphrodite with a penny in my mouth.
There is a life we live and a life we forget.
When the trees blow back and forth
in the cold November wind I think them
torsos and heads shaking wildly in my window.
Occupying, the trees do, the corner
of my eye. I can only think posthumously
these days. The fire in my heart has gone
kaput. Kaput from *être capot*—to be
without tricks in a card game. My heart
is out of tricks and the game has gone sour.
There's a beach down the street
that I never make it to. The texts gone
unanswered, the emails, the calls. *Sorry,*
I'm always chuckling. *What is one to do?*
How malleable a lifetime of displeasure
can be—Nightly, I swarm. Nightly, I consider
stars and winter mornings. I read theory
on the discursive limits of sex. Purpose! A charming
little polemic—to call a war upon
my own polytropos self. This self
that did nothing, really. The trees swerve outside.
Of course, I want to die. The trees
swerving. Nightly, I string myself up.

GESTURE
TOWARDS
IMMORTALITY

The panting of
pornography
fills an utter
      silence—
a body opens
        I want it. I want it.

I traverse, factually.

                     Though,
a bristling transformation
        does
take place. The eyes
        reassemble.
        oh yes   yes
A building sprouts.
        Pools modulate.

Encore! Encore!

Trespasser of beauty—
I want to be taken.
Taken away. Taken apart.

The screen
        shutters

like an eye-
		blink.

I strip. I strip
		down
I strip
		tease.

ur sucha tease,
		she once said.

Oblivion felt good, now
doesn't. *Don't touch me.* Months spiraled:
		—cloudy— technicolor—
	nonspecific.

In New York,
		she brushes
the hair
		on my upper lip . . .
tender
		as one might
touch
		a creature in a tank.

Two fingers—

We brainstorm
		safe words—
ocean, I say. *Ocean.* We love
		to talk.

We fuck. We lol. We admit.

ur so
abt me

asleep smelling of u

Distance breaks us down.

did u make it

did u make it
home

It's as if
     only
when in pieces
     I find
myself again.

TERMINAL
THEATER

Oh God! An evening martini
is the backdrop
to so much displeasure.
I have wanted to say this
for so long . . . Tonight I say it. Simply,
I want to be filled. Memory spills
like motor oil on the driveway.
An antelope walks across
the bright green field
of my mind. Simply, *When I say*
I love you, I mean it.
Georgia slurps you up. Here,
buildings glimmer like horns
upon a wild beast. *Buck up,*
I tell myself, *buck-up-god-dammit.*
The brackish sky fills with flight.
I could feel it,
I could feel it in the pit of me,
that you were loving her
the way you had once loved me.
I try writing
      pine trees in winter!
      snow on the city streets ....
Nothing works. Nothing
can be beautiful tonight.
The thick dream lost.

I have felt that slow gallop
of desire rise and then fall
within me. All the fucking
then all the leaving. I'm in the gutter.
The city scoffs at me! I burst at the seams.

This time the door opens. *Move*, you move.

All the windows have their curtains removed.

The glass is closed though you can see outside.

You can see the wind move through trees.

The flowers being pulled to one side. You

can't feel the wind. You're in the house.

It feels like you are outside, but you're in

the house. You're in the house. The day tips

into dusk—cocktail hour, the saddest blue.

In one room you know she is there, waiting.

There's something wrong. Something you

can't understand though you're trying.

The geckos are clicking. Crickets are starting

their naughty tune. She says something from

the other room. You hear it, but you don't

understand. When she appears in front of you

she says *Did I scare you?* You say,

You scare me all the time.

A CLOAK
YOU CANNOT
TAKE OFF.

I am both pedestrian
and animal. Sad zoo.

I find your body,
you say in a text,
so sexy.

I divide myself into quantities,
sections, pieces, almost daily.

    You text:
/ You're surprisingly strong for your size /
you so rarely take what you want /

Some things we bear proudly,

others we, simply, endure.

You call me in the morning.

Grotesquely,

not myself—
today— cannot
be seen, cannot
      be touched.

What is it earthed in me that you desire?
Or, once did—

Your hands have found a boy in the city.

  I find your body,
you said. Those words were like skin.

DOWN
BELOW

In nightmares,
there are lemons, toilettes,
and shared cigarettes. I
was my own nightmare
for most of my life.
I have found lemons, toilettes,
and shared cigarettes
to be a constant. Fine. This ain't
no walk in the park. Though,
I do walk in parks. I walk
into the middle of a big
green field. It's so scary.
These simple things.
Scary from (s)ker to swing,
jump, move. OK. I *jump*
into the middle of a big
green field. Robins
going at it
with the worms. A good
Midwest thunderstorm
creeping over the arch.
All I'm thinking is: *can you*
tell I don't have
a cock in these jeans?
Sometimes I'm missing everything.
An ex calls me *self-involved*.

What a terrible truth! But
you didn't have to say it . . .
Whatever. There are plenty of days
I don't make it out of bed. Sure.
Sure. I have let people treat
me badly. Sure. I'm very
one of a kind. Wouldn't it be cool
to live forever? Don't be
so coy. I wasted so much time
living a good life in a bad way.
I come. I breathe. I drink a beer
on the porch, alone. Perfect.
The good news is
that I fall apart all the time—
and yet, here I am
putting off, mainly, taking out
the trash. *How lucky*, I bet
you're thinking—

SELF-PORTRAIT

I track the night
over the desert. I am
all drape, today.
The intimate death
of a friend
hurtles through me.
A tube of lipstick is needed
to draw a mouth. There is
no mouth now. I cry
into the soft green velvet
of a lover's chair. A single crow
is silent on the ground. Where
is my hat? Where is my head?
I take note of my properties.
I am the colt—a sheet dancing
wildly in the wind. Then stillness.
The crow is my tie to the earth.
The night, a funeral.
There's no comfort in these things.
Why can't I see myself here?
Can you see me? I don't want to die.

CORMORANTS

There is always violence
on the brink. There is
always a violence.
Cormorants walk the beach.
Planets spin in the air.
I can see the ships
through the fog. Death
takes all the fun
out of playing. At night
a small girl dressed
in black—wings for arms—
comes to me. Her face
so obscured—I can barely
look at her. *You're burning
me*, she says. When I look
down, I am.

GRAPHIC

The wind comes through sharp as a dog growl.
There is so much shape between us.
We become another shape. We bend
in and out of being. Etcetera of hair,
brush-brown. Alternate apertures.
Where? Red and red. A drawn face
haunts like a mobile. Dawn sprouts
a violet field. Histories
are begotten then dissolve. What?
Where are you? Memory slips.
Hands immediate. Immediate
as air: dense with lip and
hand. I watch your hand
move like a flapping wing into
sullen bird.
Moths and horses occupy tongue and time.
Your eyes pollute with light: blue-flares
in the whelp of the nightroom.
Blink: a flash. Blink: a fish.
There is nothing normal about this.
We hold each other tightly— until
we do not know what we are holding.

On the bedpost there is a rope. *Lay down.*

You lay down. Sometimes a room feels pulsing,

or pretty, or both. The carpet is blue and white

with an indiscernible pattern. You can see the carpet

out of the corner of your eye. On one end

of the rope is a bedpost and on the other end

are your hands. The rope is taut and

your body is excited. The TV is on in the other

room—laugh track, mens' voices. Her hand starts

on your chest. She can feel your heart. Fast. It

stays fast. She slips a finger into your mouth.

The sun is barely lighting the room. It's dark

inside, but outside there is light. The light is leaving

fast. The light is slippery like water. It's vanishing

so quickly, the light, that night falls fast and hard.

Harder even. Your eyes are open. Have they always

been? She's on top of you. You're out of breath.

Yes you whimper. Your body aflare with hers.

INTIMACY
ABSTRACT

The cold knock of your hand
on my back. The cool balm
of the bed. A secret
in the circle of my head.
You're standing in the next room,
telling me something.
I'm at the helm of here
and not now. Once
I felt so shielded. It
was my favorite home.
You say my name.
You are in full command.
There's nothing rosy.
It's warm, but stark
and blue. It? Everything.
The door closed. A little click
of lock. A cool hand
on a hot back. Desire,
comes for lack of a better word.
It was you, who soothed
the dream. Now, the air
reminds me of the breeze!
Once felt. A breach.
A fallen hair
in the dustpan lost.
A finger over the shutter

of a Saturday night.
The smell of city-food
rising to a building's
midriff. There is something
vulnerable about laundry.
Your red shirt on the brown floor.
Soft puddle. Blur of parts.
Yes, it is then.
I kiss the back of your neck.
Warm as an apple. *Nice.*

Say lover again.
Tell me what to do.
I can become anything. I did.

EMANATION
SONG

How unequipped we are. We always are.
Stalled car outside. Metallic hum:
waiting to wail. The conscience
is gilded. The conscience
is splotched.

Imagery: pornographic hungers.
Difficult conversations.

What if I was?
If I was at all.
A shapeshift past.
I brush snow.
How easy it is
to be tender.

Stars— dandelions, guillotined.

In the dream there is abundance.
Not of stars. Not of lions. The self,
overpoured. I fall into my own horror:
late night wantings, a gruesome touch.
Having to speak it.

Dear Prince of Love,
are we all splinters

of your persona? You,
my depth. My woolen cloth.
Tell me a dreamy desire.
The world wants you in it:
undressed and beckoning.

Everything touched has been waiting.

I DESPAIR!
I DISENGAGE.

Tits perky in the cool spring. All tight and what if.
Late night. Slipshod bodies. Dark bar. The ruthless truth
of your flamboyant tongue. *You never mean to hurt me.*
Inciting honesty upthrusts a self that shudders like a spectre.
But you do hurt me. The city havoc whistling *what? what?*
Hey sir. You give me a secret kiss.
I used to know your mouth like a practiced handshake.
Now a kiss is like a hush-hush: *but I wanna.* The city lies open
like it's baring its chest at me. Brandishing. Brandishing
and beautiful. I'm breathless.

BOYHOOD

I saw something live,
it was a beautiful thing—

      and easy, like a blue jay shimmering in the light.

I stood there in the buzzing snow—
her eyes glaucopic as she sang

what if?
            what if?

into the silence.

We were living together
in this place. We shrugged
off all other truths.

It was hard at first—
      the blankness, the wanting.

Then it was all I had.

I stood still in the buzzing snow—
playing the hum of a copper opera in my mind.

What if I unknot what I need to say,

and still cannot say it?

Irresponsible. Irresistible.

An extravagant lack of an extravagant thing.

LETTER

From somewhere that is so deep into the land
the impression is like a valley,
is like a riverbed long   long   long—
TIME, sulked away.

Pile of broken glass looks green-blue,
captures something,
gives it back.
MISSHAPEN
comes up everywhere—
I see building windows.
When I open the apartment
window, to let the air in, it is your chest
coming through your blouse.

Murky, murky, mind!
Oh, *Xanthum*, a pretty word— useless.
Messages form around roofs and doorknobs—
see them everywhere. There's a crisis inside.

the feeling of water
that makes you vulnerable
high   wind

What would you say if I said *love is clear like glass!*
Only say what you mean:

Polka-dot

Polka-dot

Sheep in red coats line our insides.

I'm kind and I'm kind of.

If we could be birds simply by flapping our arms like wings we would do so, we would love the air and call it: *our air.* Language can hold us together even when we cannot hold ourselves.

Really, you are my favorite doorway.

The flowers glower in the heat (smell: sweet-sweet-sweet), air slow, slow is everywhere, things are and are moving. All the green rustles: slow waves, various shades. Red-house-top (a mountain)— sky, unusually pale. Your hair is wet and smooth, kelp, but darker. *Come* you say, and I come.

In the morning you drive a car. The car is black
and the sky is black. The sky is dark, then, erupts into
something dangerous. You are always going
where one must go. Music plays. You're going
somewhere important and your stomach feels
tight. When you walk into a room often you imagine
you're a better person than you are. She
loved you no matter what. People on the sidewalk
don't care about you at all. There's a comfort
in both. You want someone to get up from their
seat. Hold you against the wall. Fuck you until
the sky goes dark or the mind blankens. Blank
as snowfall untouched in the morning when you
go to the car. Blank as the sea or the sand or the
grey desk in front of you. To your left you see
the sky. *Dangerous.* The phone rings.
It rings like it wants something from you.
Ring. Ring. You want to be held against
the wall. To shudder. Ring. Ring. To fall inside.
To fall very deep.

DIRT

It was the grey cat with the robin in his mouth,
or you flicking your cigarette off the porch—
that first warm night of April—when I began
wondering how this would all pan out. This all
meaning nothing other than you and I, our
languished urge to be jointed. Hidden from
the sense of things—is our leitmotif
of daily-drama. A man plays the fiddle
and a skateboarder speaks loud French. Day
whisps off into another cast-iron night. Night
makes all too clear our real bad burdens.
I shuck my burdens for some universal truth—
truth never being the balm it should—I come
out empty-handed. One time, early, before
you had heard some damp secret
from my screwball past, you sat on my lap
in your big pink robe wielding a glass of wine.
We spoke only of Southern tics and surefire
obscurities. We each let our voices sprawl out
over the silent swamp of all we could not know.
I don't know you at all, you said.
The swamp grew deeper then. Or longer.
You come into the kitchen when I call you—
your hands scooping up a beetle gentle as ash.
Ash falls often from where I'm standing.
The beetles never flutter—just crawl

unromantically across the soft brown tiles.
Nowhere to go! Nowhere to be! I sing out.
The thing is when I say your name,
you always answer. And when you say mine,
it's like a door slamming shut. The cicadas
will start any day now—their voices forming
like a thick wool cloth through the air.
That collective voice rubs up against you—
gets in your shirt and your head. I want
to be so unseen it hurts sometimes.
If I could be dirt,
I would.

EMINENCE

It wasn't perfect, this place—
nor our life—though, it had
still felt like it all could be.

When we spoke, at first,
we said things like *fireflies*
      brim the deceit of power.

We were lonely, really.
That's what we meant
anyhow. One night

there was no moon. It was so dark
and we couldn't see
the other side to things.

As time passed (gradually
then all at once) we began
to speak:

      hot gravel hot gravel
I'm so hurt

Racoons hunted. Vultures circled
some unknown tragedy. A deer
stood at the other side of the spring.

It was the last night, though,
cooler than all the rest,
an incredible harshness—

our voices mirroring a perfect harmony—
you're selfish   insecure / play-
the-victim
   hotheaded you're greedy
a liar

Who isn't, who hasn't? It was the least
beautiful thing about us. How steadfast
we hid behind the truth. The truth didn't matter.

What did we really want?
To break, to not be the broken-one, anymore.

THE
ORCHARD

I have no glamor. I want
       to go quietly.

Like an apple growing on a tree.

Or a cloud blowing
across the evening sky.

What is this
choking silence? What is
       this reflection
in a glass? The microwave
       beeps. The phone
lets out a buzz. The skyline
       is dark and steady.

A fruit fly haunts at the window.

Faith?
Belief?
The things we fill
       our time with.

When I open my mouth
it's like an empty fridge.
When I open the apartment door
            there's nowhere to be.

She said:

            I would've been there for all of it.

All of it meaning: even this. How come
I couldn't love her? No.
Some things just don't make sense.

UNTITLED
NATURE
STUDY

After Hilma Klint

The thing is I make a line
and I follow it. Sometimes:
a cross, but inverted. Hell,

                a hillside.
It matters and then it stops. I desire
to dominate. Mosses. Mirrors. Memory.
In perfection I long to show power,

           then plainness.
A field as blank as a cheek.
I have always thought: mosquito
is an abstract shape. Algae, anemone,
too. Dangerous thoughts
spill— green-grey, unedged.
This is the world I call home,
then nature. Viola odorata—
emblematic scent of sex. Saturnalia
of candid ignorance. We enter
the world just once and then another.
Take up a shell. A swan-shadow.

We bloom. We say: *good night.*
Meaning: pick me: I reek of want.

FANTASY

I wanted to break apart each day—
in front of you. Though, I stood
still like a reed. Sunshine.
Speaking in the daylight.
Normalcy, normalcy. I wore a shirt
with buttons. I spoke in boring
passages.

At night I crawl into bed
alone; sometimes when night
is at its deepest and the train rattles
the house like a wave passing
through a boat—I see myself
with such odd precision
it shakes me and I shake out
all the bad things I've done to myself.

Some days you are in a field. Others the street,
the beach. You have known many things to be
true—the sunrise, the sunset, birds are hungry,
you step out of bed always with caution. These
are the things you hold close. One day you
get on your hands and knees. It seems like a field
though it's your bed. It feels like a beach though
it can't be. She says *Are you ready?* You're always
ready. You cannot believe the things you want.
Outside a car is locked, locked again. Caution.
Entering you. Entering you, again. Voices whip
through the alleyway. *Yes* you say, *yes*, until
you don't mean it anymore. You cannot think.
Silverfish. Patio. *Yes, yes.* This changes nothing.
She pulls out. It's like drowning. You can't breathe.
Yes, you're saying, *yes* as you pull on your sweater.
Yes, *yes* as you leave, and *yes* you're thinking
even when the day has completely slipped
into another one entirely.

THIS PLACE
IS CALLED
BEULAH

There is a place where Contrarieties are equally True
This place is called Beulah, It is a pleasant lovely Shadow
Where no dispute can come, Because of those who Sleep.
—William Blake

The lake was blue pastoral,
and it was clear and my face
was inside it next to yours.

I said: *look at this blue*
Pastoral landscape!
You looked into my eyes and smiled.

Once, I considered
that pastoral could be
past and oral, not sexually,

of course, but traditionally,
A Past Oral Tradition,
though— it is— Romantic—

The sun burned us into brighter
animals.

I'll follow you, I had wished to say,
as you submerged into
the simple dazzle of lakewater.

You disappeared. You shepherded
me so far away from my self
that I do not feel at home

there any longer. I watch
who I am becoming
swim out across the water,

and stand next to where you unfold.
Blue heron, you said.
Blue errand, I heard.
It was like I had never heard you before.

TWO CHILDREN THREATENED BY A NIGHTINGALE

Attracted to the guise,
and not the object.
Light coming or going,
creates a time of day.
This happened. This did happen.
If the story is about a woman,
let us call her *Arc*.
The story goes—fruit flies, horses,
delinquent power. Or the story
goes—a burning, a burning,
there is no more house.
When I speak of gentleness,
I speak of desire. What
does the nightingale have
that I don't have?
Position? Relief? I am tired
of attraction. A snake moves
across dried leaves.
I wish for a doorway.
If I was the Prince of Birds,
who could hurt me?
You couldn't.

AND THEN WE SAW
THE DAUGHTER
OF THE MINOTAUR

The clouds came into the room.
The dogs were asleep on the floor.
When I looked for something solid,
everything popped, then disappeared.
The cloak, like salmon, slid
to the ground. A song
of gossip played and played.
There was a time I wanted nothing
more than stillness. All I got
was more *want*. The want
beseeched me. I worked hard.
I undressed at night.
When visited, I was interpreted—
fragmentarily.
Nobody sees me.
The vine curls up the stone pillar.
The yellow tablecloth, wrinkles.
I pick up my cloak.
You can marvel at me. I am marvelous.
Look at me again—my back to the night.

ISLAND
OF
CALYPSO

The roadkill-deer has its neck
slung back— nose to spine—
throat taut, the skin
unbroken, but barely.

I'd say it was swooning
aristocratically. Graceful—
balletic. When we first met,
you would text me:
u make me swoon. Of course,
I would think: *u make me swan*.
B/c? Why not? I revel
in false cognates—
An aesthetic bird, the swan.
Aggressive. Violent. Beautiful.
The soft hook of its neck
still as marble
in the autumn breeze. Romantic,
really. *u make me swoon too*—
We fall. The roads rouge.

The dead deer are everywhere—
as I drive home from up north.
Everything flat. The sky
pink as girlhood and purple
like an adult bruise. I'm overcome

with the desire to reach
my arms out and sing a pop
song into the crepuscular eve!
I make myself sad with how
sad I am. A deer and then another.
It's not the deer I'm talking of,
but the gesture,
the way you'd make me fold.
Then the way you'd fold for me.
Our necks slinging back
in bed. We left
each other folded over.
It's like our bodies
meant nothing and the world
just kept turning.

In the days that followed many words were
said. *You had to have known.* You had to
have known. You enter a stranger's house
per their instructions. You get into bed.
Oblivion. A bed is like a harbor. Anything
can happen. Anything can hurt you. If you
want to be hurt? You can wear your
pain like a badge upon your shoulder.
If you want to be hurt you can live
through anything. *What do you mean?*
A voice is asking, is asking every day.
I don't mean anything, I don't mean
anything by it. You're almost shouting.
The truth so close to your lips. You take notes:
blue armchair, dripping faucet, three cans
on the coffee table, blue sheets, blue
blankets, blue coat. You wish to wear
oblivion like a coat. *You don't mean anything,*
the voice says back, almost laughing now.

NOSTOS

Lake reflects sky,
sky reflects the razzle-dazzle
of blue and blue.

Somewhere between the warp of land
and air there's your body
and someone else
beside it.

Birds come and go—

up   and down   forward   then back

Blue jays like broken sky,
crows like drips of night,
songbirds howling
into the oblivious myth.

Yellow jackets too
swirl off somewhere,
then away. Farther
cicadas sing: *Tu me manques, tu me manques*
aussi   you are missing from me

It *is* theatrical— this loss,

this losing. We fall
into tragedy. Goat-song.   Meaning
has gotten lost   along our way.

I pale in the face.   You are
un   reachable.

I hold a dark lake in my hand.   I wait

for light   to seethe across   the surface.

Where are you? The wind   is sky beginning.
I can see it form for miles.
Do you feel it? The way it moves around you
then on.

Fall rain, the horizon.

                Something

is broken.   This breaking

        happens once

                then happens all the time.

CASTLES

Once, I watched the ocean rise up
on its miraculous haunches,
blue and cursed to fall within itself

forever. I was a child
and frightened by power. I listened
and opened doors for strangers.

There is a certain dread that comes
along with being human. We are castles
of what? Patterns and sex?

I know I am destroying the romance
of this all. *I hope you got everything
you wanted—* the nurse said as I left.

I imagine, we listen to others
when we fail ourselves.

This, though, was never quite failure.
The world flexed, and I was flown—
my body aching
for the anatomy of boyhood.

ANTEROOM

The overhead light makes a mirror
of the last words said.
I sit in the empty room.

People down on the sidewalk are still
sputtering hot— laughter.
Car bells. Shutdoors. Something

glows in a blue cloud:
at a loss. A word before,
some after. Lost, anyhow.

My Tyger has burnt out. My *Tyger*
has *burnt* out. Alas, I come to undress

my point, once, this was all for you.

The egret inhabits an estuary, back
home in California. Oh, but the egress

is available forthright and waiting
with its open yowl. Too soon.
I wish to curtail my time.

The pure Punctum of your hair—
like silvered-brown— still thick

and turning between

the fingers of my stupid hand.
The skin of your eyes like lore
glass. Nothing else, but blue.

Where has our gondolier gone?
The boat rocking against
the urchined water— perpetual.

Empty space can feel full
and neon. There was once
the simplicity of us. The air

wreaked of rain and dirt.
What was that then? The sad
depth of your hand, right there.

In the morning the snow is dust, snowdust.
In the morning there is a lone body
on the sidewalk. The body is walking
towards you. The streetlights casting a
weak glow. Dawn sputtering. Daylight
grizzling above the pines. The body
moves like it is scared of you. You stay
very still like you're scared too. You can
taste wine from last night still on your
breath. You brush snow from your windows.
Slowly. You're touching everything slowly.
Your hands are numbing, but you don't stop.
In the car the heat feels good. The heat
feels good in the morning. *Where am*
I going? Last night, you let her do what
she wanted. What she wanted became
what you wanted. There's a bruise on
your body. You feel it against your shirt.
There's a bruise on your body like a pool.
Inside the bruise you put the memory. It
wades in and never comes out.

TRANS
IS LATIN
FOR ACROSS

Across, as in: over there, beyond.

The phrase *life-expectancy*
isn't sexy, per se.
Though it is beautiful
to have a life—and a love.
Even when I think:
I wish I could be
only a freakout,
only crossing the street.

I suppose: there is a sense
and there is a nonsense
to what it feels like to be.

I pose. I compose.
In a trans way, of course.

I can't listen to sad music.
Please, don't make me.
When I take off my shirt
in the mirror— it too, isn't
sexy. Or, rarely, is it sexy.
I cry, and that's the truth.

One past love

pushed me
against the wall,
said: *do you want to feel*
       like a man?

Sure. There was
a summer storm.
We fucked for hours.
Then, she smoked,
while I slept. Simple.

It's not that I became
anything. I was, I was.
And I slept. And I sleep.

It is nothing special
to not want to be hurt.

Notes

But of course, there is a movement—The small fragment that starts the collection is a loose erasure of Hugo Ball's *The Dada Manifesto*.

"The History" references "The Fly" by William Blake as well as a point made by Hazard Adams in his book *William Blake: A Reading of the Shorter Poems*. I wrote this poem in tandem with an essay called "William Blake: Blakean Prosody in Twenty-First Century Poetics"—one of the relationships I consider is Blake's "The Fly" with Aditi Machado's poem "If Thought Is" that ends her first collection, *Some Beheadings*.

"Lips crash with lips inevitable," the title is a nod to "Metaphor for Action" by Muriel Rukeyser. I was thinking of barnacles after reading "Hang On" by Rae Armantrout in the *New Yorker* that morning.

"The Lovers" refers to *Dante's Inferno*, specifically to canto II and canto V—from the former I borrow the line *You must know this: what it is to doubt* and from the latter the line *Until a moment did us in* (both from Mary Jo Bang's excellent translation). The line that follows in canto II is: "As one who revises his idea of what he wants," which, though not in my poem, certainly thematically speaks to it. Additionally, this wonderful Latin word, "occulatae," is used in *On the Marriage of Philology and Mercury* by Martianus Capella to describe the robe of Jupiter—thought to perhaps be a reference to a peacocked pattern. I was struck by the way this term can suggest the horrifying idea of a cloak literally covered in eyes as well as the symbolism of the eye ("all-seeing").

I wrote "Stage Directions" with the balcony door open during a very hard thunderstorm in the midst of summer with my chair right up at the edge of the doorway—warm, and raining, and loud, while drinking this funny little spritzer. I mention this because the poem acts very much like a doorway to me, a portal—something that gives way to two sides (innocence and experience, comfort and violence, inside and outside). The mention of Perec happens to be in reference to my girlfriend reading *W, or the Memory of Childhood*. The "one guy" who once said *get used to using each other* is Ted Berrigan (from one of his sonnets). When I say "bad urns" I'm thinking of Laura Jensen's "Bad Boats." Lastly, *course-core-coarse-corps-body-death* was a note Aditi Machado wrote on the board when I visited her class that I copied into my notebook.

"Medusa": *Oh I'll tell you about a complicated man* is a reference to the Odyssey. It is essentially the first line of *The Odyssey* in book 1 ("The Boy and the Goddess"), the first line being "Tell me about a complicated man." The pig began as a reference to "Love Songs" by Mina Loy where she has this line "Pig Cupid his rosy snout"—though the pig became a more singular pig than only referential.

"Self-Portrait (Punching Ball)" is the first of a handful of ekphrastic poems on work by Leonora Carrington and Max Ernst. This one references Ernst's *Le Punching Ball ou l'Immortalité de Buonarroti*.

"Corydon to Alexis": The names Corydon and Alexis refer to Virgil's second eclogue.

"Sphinx": The question *how do you see me anyways?* is the pivotal question in the novel *Sphinx* by Anne Garréta. The sphinx is in some cultures a man, in others a woman, and, of course, known for asking a riddle that one must answer—in order to get past the creature, the monster. "Nobodaddy" is a figure in William Blake's mythology—essentially a false god ("Father of Jealousy"). Interestingly, besides the obvious etymology of the name being a collapsed form of the phrase "nobody's daddy," it is also, "a close anagram of the name of a character who appears in two of Blake's favorite Biblical books, Job and Revelation: Abaddon (Hebrew for 'destruction'). Anagrammatized, 'Abaddon' becomes 'Nobadad.' He is 'the angel of the bottomless pit' who appears in Revelation 9:11 and is mentioned in Job 26:6" (L. Edwin Folsom, "Nobodaddy: Through the Bottomless Pit, Darkly," *Blake/An Illustrated Quarterly*, Volume 9, Issue 2, Fall 1975, pp. 45–46). Nobodaddy is also an iteration of Urizen, which I quote in the epigraph of the collection.

"Down Below" is a dual ekphrastic poem of the written piece *Down Below* and the painting by the same name—both by Leonora Carrington.

"The Wolves": The italicized moment, *I don't know what are a body and hands a mouth a sex*, is from *The Obscene Madame D* by Hilda Hilst.

"The Scholar": The Greek word "polytropos" is the first adjective given to Odysseus—it means "much traveled, much wandering" but also "crafty"; in one translation it's "the man of twists and turns." *Poly-*, of course, means "many, multiple" while *tropos* literally translates to "turn." Emily Wilson ruminates on the term in an interview in the *New York Times*—considering whether the term is meant to suggest that Odysseus is passive in that he's been "turned off" the straight path (to home) by the gods, monsters, etc., *or* that, as she says, he's "the turner" meaning he's untrustworthy, "turns" a situation to his advantage.

"Terminal Theater" borrows its title from a poem by the same name in *Kissing the Dancer* by Robert Sward. It ends phenomenally with, "What is real? cried the oyster, glob of spit / In a pane of glass."

"Self-Portrait" is an ekphrasis of Leonora Carrington's painting *Self-Portrait in Orthopedic Black Tie*.

"Cormorants" is an ekphrasis of Max Ernst's *Cormorants*.

"Graphic" was originally titled "Rayograph" and was meant to look at a memory as a photogram. I was particularly considering Man Ray's photogram included within *L'ange Heurtebise* by Jean Cocteau.

"Emanation Song" and "I despair! I disengage.": Blake's "four-fold man." Essentially, "Emanations" are the feminine counterpart of the four-fold man (though in Eternity sexual division is obsolete). One of the facts that interests me most about Emanations is what Blake says in *Jerusalem*: "[Emanations] stand both Male and Female at the Gates of each Humanity." While the "Spectre" represents what's been called "the self-centered Selfhood"—it is the Rational power (as opposed to, say, Imaginative power). The Spectre dwells in the chaos of memory (as Blake "clarifies" in *Jerusalem*). In my opinion, it symbolizes both the power and danger of the individual's "self" and the effects, and potential, in acting in one's self-interest.

In "Boyhood" the word "glaucopic" is a reference to *Glaukopis,* the epithet associated with Athena in Homer's work (meaning *bright-eyed*—it originally meant silvery, though now it refers to something more blue).

"Untitled Nature Study" is "in conversation with" the work of Hilma Klint— particularly the book on her notes and methods.

"This place is called Beulah": Beulah is a particular landscape within the Blakean mythos. The poem's epigraph describes it well. In a delightful happenstance, it is also the name of a small town in Michigan where I spent a brief but memorable time.

"Two Children Threatened by a Nightingale": *Two Children Are Threatened by a Nightingale* is perhaps the most famous painting by Max Ernst.

"And Then We Saw the Daughter of the Minotaur" takes the title from a painting by Leonora Carrington—"I was interpreted fragmentarily" is said by

Carrington in *Down Below*.

"Island of Calypso": To make a long story short—Calypso is the nymph who enchants Odysseus.

"Nostos," the term, is a theme used in Ancient Greek literature, which includes an epic hero returning home by sea. The poem itself is indebted to Marie Howe's "You Think This Happened Only Once and Long Ago."

A note on the unnamed poems: I am very interested in the constant issue that we live two lives—the public life and the private life—and that these two converge and diverge at important apexes. It's not that these represent a different story but a parallel one—an unfolding amid what is already unfolding, though not always the central topic of conversation. In Greek tragedy there is the stasimon, which is "a stationary song" that the chorus sings. This may be a useful concept to consider when thinking structurally how these come to be *interludes* or *disruptions*—that they come in a history of a similar praxis.

Acknowledgements & Gratitude

Thank you to the following publications, where some of these poems have appeared:

Afternoon Visitor, "Terminal Theater" & "Icarus"

AGNI, "Down Below"

Berkeley Poetry Review, "Letter," "Graphic," & "Anteroom"

Best Buds! Collective, "The Cave"

Burnside Review, "Automania"

The Boiler, "Boyhood" and "Requiem Circuit"

DREGINALD, "Gesture towards Immortality," "Emanation Song," & "I despair! I disengage."

Ghost City Review, "Of Figure and Field"

Indiana Review, "Sphinx"

jubilat, "A cloak you cannot take off."

Nat. Brut, "Nostos" (previously, "You Having Been")

The Offing, "Intimacy Abstract" & "City-Builders" (previously, "I kiss the fire in your hands, or City Builders")

Pinwheel, "Days pass like perfume," "In the days that followed," and "In the morning the snow is dust"

pulpmouth, "The History"

Redivider, "Island of Calypso" (previously, "Enter the Ghost")

Sip Cup, "Self-Portrait" (previously, "Self-Portrait in Orthopedic Black Tie")

Sixth Finch, "Trans Is Latin for Across."

Tin House, "This place is called Beulah"

Sections from "Fantasy" were used in the song "The fire's gone out" arranged by Baldwin Giang, sung by Vidita Kanniks, and put to piano by Georgia Mills.

Firstly, I want to thank my poetry teachers for their incredible generosity and patience and belief—truly, this book would not be here without them: Mary Szybist, Jerry Harp, Carl Phillips, and Mary Jo Bang. Thanks as well as to my other teachers in varying genres who inspired, supported, and encouraged me throughout the years: Kathryn Davis, Marty Riker, Kathleen Finneran, francine j. harris, Natasha Trethewey, and Kurt Fosso.

A special thanks to my cohort at Washington University in St. Louis: Colin Criss, Victoria Hsu, Paul Tran, and Emma Wilson.

To my many friends, colleagues, and acquaintances who read, said, listened, despaired, and laughed with me over the years. All of your enthusiasm, critiques, and ideas—I am eternally grateful: Red Samaniego, Analeah Rosen, Halley Perry, Aditi Machado, Billy Youngblood, Meagan Cass, Sanam Sheriff, Cassie Donish, Kelly Caldwell, Serena Solin, Luther Hughes, Emily Pittinos, Christina Wood Martinez, Jordan Keller-Martinez, Miranda Popkey, and Emi Noguchi.

To my family, Bobbye, Todd, Elmer, Amy, and, especially, my mom, Alyson Yarberry.

S. Yarberry is a trans poet and writer. Their poetry has appeared in *Tin House, Indiana Review, The Offing, Berkeley Poetry Review, jubilat,* among others. Their other writings can be found in *Bomb Magazine, The Adroit Journal,* and *Blake/An Illustrated Quarterly.* They currently serve as the Poetry Editor of *The Spectacle.* S. has their MFA in Poetry from Washington University in St. Louis and is a PhD candidate at Northwestern University where they are a Mellon Cluster Fellow in Poetry & Poetics.

Thank you all
for your support.
We do this for you,
and could not do
it without you.

DEEP
VELLUM

PARTNERS

pixel ||| texel

LIFE
IN DEEP ELLUM

EMBREY FAMILY
FOUNDATION

COMMON
DESK
COWORKING

ALLRED
CAPITAL MANAGEMENT
of
RAYMOND JAMES®

ADDITIONAL DONORS, CONT'D

Mark Haber
Mary Cline
Maynard Thomson
Michael Reklis
Mike Soto
Mokhtar Ramadan
Nikki & Dennis Gibson
Patrick Kukucka
Patrick Kutcher
Rev. Elizabeth & Neil Moseley
Richard Meyer

Scott & Katy Nimmons
Sherry Perry
Sydneyann Binion
Stephen Harding
Stephen Williamson
Susan Carp
Susan Ernst
Theater Jones
Tim Perttula
Tony Thomson

SUBSCRIBERS

Ned Russin
Michael Binkley
Michael Schneiderman
Aviya Kushner
Kenneth McClain
Eugenie Cha
Stephen Fuller
Joseph Rebella
Brian Matthew Kim

Anthony Brown
Michael Lighty
Erin Kubatzky
Shelby Vincent
Margaret Terwey
Ben Fountain
Caroline West
Ryan Todd
Gina Rios

Caitlin Jans
Ian Robinson
Elena Rush
Courtney Sheedy
Elif Ağanoğlu
Laura Gee
Valerie Boyd
Brian Bell

AVAILABLE NOW FROM DEEP VELLUM

MARIA GABRIELA LLANSOL · *The Geography of Rebels Trilogy: The Book of Communities; The Remaining Life; In the House of July & August* · translated by Audrey Young · PORTUGAL

PABLO MARTÍN SÁNCHEZ · *The Anarchist Who Shared My Name* · translated by Jeff Diteman · SPAIN

DOROTA MASŁOWSKA · *Honey, I Killed the Cats* · translated by Benjamin Paloff · POLAND

BRICE MATTHIEUSSENT· *Revenge of the Translator* · translated by Emma Ramadan · FRANCE

LINA MERUANE · *Seeing Red* · translated by Megan McDowell · CHILE

VALÉRIE MRÉJEN · *Black Forest* · translated by Katie Shireen Assef · FRANCE

FISTON MWANZA MUJILA · *Tram 83* · *The River in the Belly: Selected Poems* · translated by Bret Maney DEMOCRATIC REPUBLIC OF CONGO

GORAN PETROVÍC · *At the Lucky Hand, aka The Sixty-Nine Drawers* · translated by Peter Agnone · SERBIA

LUDMILLA PETRUSHEVSKAYA · *The New Adventures of Helen: Magical Tales* · translated by Jane Bugaeva · RUSSIA

ILJA LEONARD PFEIJFFER · *La Superba* · translated by Michele Hutchison · NETHERLANDS

RICARDO PIGLIA · *Target in the Night* · translated by Sergio Waisman · ARGENTINA

SERGIO PITOL · *The Art of Flight* · *The Journey* · *The Magician of Vienna* · *Mephisto's Waltz: Selected Short Stories* · *The Love Parade* · translated by George Henson · MEXICO

JULIE POOLE · *Bright Specimen: Poems from the Texas Herbarium* · USA

EDUARDO RABASA · *A Zero-Sum Game* · translated by Christina MacSweeney · MEXICO

ZAHIA RAHMANI · *"Muslim": A Novel* · translated by Matthew Reeck · FRANCE/ALGERIA

MANON STEFAN ROS · *The Blue Book of Nebo* · WALES

JUAN RULFO · *The Golden Cockerel & Other Writings* · translated by Douglas J. Weatherford · MEXICO

ETHAN RUTHERFORD · *Farthest South & Other Stories* · USA

TATIANA RYCKMAN · *Ancestry of Objects* · USA

JIM SCHUTZE · *The Accommodation* · USA

OLEG SENTSOV · *Life Went On Anyway* · translated by Uilleam Blacker · UKRAINE

MIKHAIL SHISHKIN · *Calligraphy Lesson: The Collected Stories* · translated by Marian Schwartz, Leo Shtutin, Mariya Bashkatova, Sylvia Maizell · RUSSIA

ÓFEIGUR SIGURÐSSON · *Öræfi: The Wasteland* · translated by Lytton Smith · ICELAND

DANIEL SIMON, ED. · *Dispatches from the Republic of Letters* · USA

MUSTAFA STITOU · *Two Half Faces* · translated by David Colmer · NETHERLANDS

SOPHIA TERAZAWA · *Winter Phoenix: Testimonies in Verse* · POLAND

MÄRTA TIKKANEN · *The Love Story of the Century* · translated by Stina Katchadourian · SWEDEN

BOB TRAMMELL · *Jack Ruby & the Origins of the Avant-Garde in Dallas & Other Stories* · USA

BENJAMIN VILLEGAS · *ELPASO: A Punk Story* · translated by Jay Noden · MEXICO

SERHIY ZHADAN · *Voroshilovgrad* · translated by Reilly Costigan-Humes & Isaac Wheeler · UKRAINE

FORTHCOMING FROM DEEP VELLUM

MARIO BELLATIN • *Etchapare* • translated by Shook • MEXICO

CAYLIN CARPA-THOMAS • *Iguana Iguana* • USA

MIRCEA CĂRTĂRESCU • *Solenoid* • translated by Sean Cotter • ROMANIA

TIM COURSEY • *Driving Lessons* • USA

ANANDA DEVI • *When the Night Agrees to Speak to Me* • translated by Kazim Ali •
MAURITIUS

DHUMKETU • *The Shehnai Virtuoso* • translated by Jenny Bhatt • INDIA

LEYLÂ ERBIL • *A Strange Woman* •
translated by Nermin Menemencioğlu & Amy Marie Spangler • TURKEY

ALLA GORBUNOVA • *It's the End of the World, My Love* •
translated by Elina Alter • RUSSIA

NIVEN GOVINDEN • *Diary of a Film* • GREAT BRITAIN

GYULA JENEI • *Always Different* • translated by Diana Senechal · HUNGARY

DIA JUBAILI • *No Windmills in Basra* • translated by Chip Rosetti • IRAQ

ELENI KEFALA • *Time Stitches* • translated by Peter Constantine • CYPRUS

UZMA ASLAM KHAN • *The Miraculous True History of Nomi Ali* • PAKISTAN

ANDREY KURKOV • *Grey Bees* • translated by Boris Dralyuk • UKRAINE

JORGE ENRIQUE LAGE • *Freeway La Movie* • translated by Lourdes Molina • CUBA

TEDI LÓPEZ MILLS • *The Book of Explanations* • translated by Robin Myers • MEXICO

ANTONIO MORESCO • *Clandestinity* • translated by Richard Dixon • ITALY

FISTON MWANZA MUJILA • *The Villain's Dance* • translated by Roland Glasser •
DEMOCRATIC REPUBLIC OF CONGO

N. PRABHAKARAN • *Diary of a Malayali Madman* •
translated by Jayasree Kalathil • INDIA

THOMAS ROSS • *Miss Abracadabra* • USA

IGNACIO RUIZ-PÉREZ • *Isles of Firm Ground* • translated by Mike Soto • MEXICO

LUDMILLA PETRUSHEVSKAYA • *Kidnapped: A Crime Story* •
translated by Marian Schwartz • RUSSIA

NOAH SIMBLIST, ed. • *Tania Bruguera: The Francis Effect* • CUBA

S. YARBERRY • *A Boy in the City* • USA